Quit Living

For Sunday

Pastor Norman Edmonds Sr.

Quit Living For Sunday

Copyright ©2016 Norman Edmonds Sr.
All Rights Reserved.

ISBN: **978-1533507983**

Published by: Kelly Publishing 2016

No part of this book may be reproduced, stored in a retrieval system or transmitted by any means without written permission from the publisher except for brief quotations in critical reviews or articles.

Unless otherwise noted Scripture quotations are from the New King James Version. Used by Permission. Scripture quotations marked ASV are from the American Standard Bible Copyright. Scripture quotations marked HCSB are from the Holman Christian Standard Bible. Scripture quotations marked AMP are from The Amplified Bible Copyright © 1954, 1958, 1962, 1964, 1965, 1987 by The Lockman Foundation. All Rights Reserved. Used by Permission.

TABLE OF CONTENTS

DEDICATION 5

INTRODUCTION 6

CHAPTERS

CHAPTER 1 – "Saved for a Day" 10

CHAPTER 2 – "This Is Hard!" 16

CHAPTER 3 – "I'm Only Human!" 21

CHAPTER 4 – "Will It Work for Me?" 26

CHAPTER 5 – "Yeah, but When?" 31

CHAPTER 6 – "It's Contagious!" 37

CHAPTER 7 – "You Make It Sound So Easy" 44

CHAPTER 8 – "This Is not What I Expected" 52

CHAPTER 9 – "What Did You Go There For?" 58

CHAPTER 10 – "Try It; You Might Like It" 64

CHAPTER 11 – "I Just Don't Feel Like It!" 71

CHAPTER 12 – "Fully Committed" 78

CHAPTER 13 – "What Am I Getting out of This? 86

CHAPTER 14 – "Don't Trip; I Got This!" 90

CHAPTER 15 – "New and Improved" 94

Preview of Follow-Up Book: **The Paint is Peeling** 99

About The Author 102

Dedication

As in all things, I give God thanks. I give all the honor and praise to my Lord and Savior Jesus Christ, for allowing me to complete this project. I thank Him, for the divine inspiration and revelation to write this book. I am humbled by the experience of being used as His vessel to speak into the lives of His people. More importantly, I am grateful to God for the manner in which the writing of this book has caused me to do some personal reflection. Therefore, I dedicate this book to My God!

I also want to dedicate this book to my amazing wife, Jeanie M. Edmonds, who is always supportive and encouraging in all that I do. To my two wonderful children—Norman Jr. and Janay Carolyn—who have helped and pushed me in so many ways, I thank you as well. I want to acknowledge my loving parents, Whitney Jr. and Clara Edmonds for always believing in me and all my siblings for the strong bond that we share. I am also thankful to the Beulah Baptist Church family of Gibson, Louisiana whom God has allowed me to pastor for the past thirteen years.

In Loving Memory

My dear sister, Carolyn E. Knight

My beloved father-in-law, Willie Washington, Jr.

Introduction

It is the power of our faith that compels millions of us to gather at local worship sites on a weekly basis. It is the aftermath of a week of struggles, disappointments, exhausting challenges and spiritual battles of the week that make the church even more of a welcomed sight as well as a place of refuge, rest, and restoration.

We enter the church doors with great anticipation. We view this as our time of relief as well as release. In **1ˢᵗ Peter 5:7**, it says, *"Casting all your care upon Him for He cares for you."* Sunday service becomes our opportunity to take full advantage of this scripture. A time of liberation from the heavy burdens we've carried throughout the week.

Now is our time to escape the overwhelming circumstances of our lives. However, we fail to realize that our faith must be lived out in our everyday experiences. For it is through the storms of life that faith is created and, at other times, enhanced.

How many times have you found yourself rushing the week by in order to get to Sunday? Many people find themselves saying, "I can't wait to get to church to get a Word." Sunday has now become our medicine for whatever is ailing us. Soon, we find ourselves living for Sunday.

At this point, some people are wondering how relevant this book is to their relationship with God. If your entire spiritual existence can be contained in a single, weekly worship service, then you are probably living for Sunday. If the totality of your faith can be reduced to the time spent inside of the four walls of a sanctuary, it is necessary for you to evaluate your relationship with God.

This book was written to challenge you to "Quit Living for Sunday!" This title sets forth a quandary that is shared by many well-meaning, Sunday-go-to-church folk. These people are those who seek the power, presence, and manifestation of miracles, while they are gathered together in that sacred place. Many times, unfortunately, they fail to realize that these events can also occur on a one to one basis and outside of the church building. The key to this evolution transpiring is for a person to develop a one to one relationship with God. This takes more than a once a week or occasional visit to church, more than a half-hearted commitment to God's way of living. Therefore, it's necessary for us to change our thought process, which will lead to a change in our actions.

Your new challenge is to live through Sunday! My purpose is to teach you that church is more than a Sunday activity. It is preparation for a Monday through Sunday responsibility. When we allow Sunday service, especially the preached Word of God, to become a shaping and refining tool, it gives us a greater chance of success.

My endeavor is to change the way you view Sunday service. It is much greater than your opportunity to pour out your heart to God. The service must be more than a time to gather with other members or to hear some uplifting songs. You must focus on allowing God to fill your heart with His presence and His Word that will guide your life in the right direction. The Lord will manifest Himself every day of your life and in every area of your life. Then you won't have to live for Sunday, but every day will become a day of spiritual renewal.

Quit Living For Sunday

Chapter 1

Saved for a Day

What necessitates a book of this nature is that most Christians, in some way or another, fail to conduct themselves as saved folk consistently. We are all guilty of this to some degree. This failure can come in the form of corrupt communication, unruly behavior, bad attitudes, unclean thoughts, etc. Sometimes these sinful offenses are so obvious and easily noted. And, at other times, they are very subtle and cunning. No matter the form in which they manifest, these behaviors are contrary to the lifestyle of a Believer.

I know it almost becomes an achievement if we can stay saved for a day. Considering the world in which we live, we do well if we can behave like a Christian for a twenty-four hour period. God calls for more. He wants every day and not just a day.

Remember the Sabbath and keep it holy—one of the Ten Commandments that many Christians take very literally. They hallow that day or at least a portion of it. While they are confined to the sanctuary, they exude an attitude of holiness, which quickly dissipates with the benediction. There seems to exist a flawed understanding of this fourth commandment. It was and is a sign of God's covenant with Israel. Since the word "Sabbath" means rest, it was and is a command which governed the days of work and the time for rest. During this rest day, the worship of God took place as well as a reflection on Israel's deliverance from bondage. Since, at that time, the Sabbath was celebrated on Saturday, someone may be saying, why does this concept find a place in a book entitled, *Quit Living for Sunday*?

Well, I'm glad you ask that question, to which there is a very simple answer. We have to get beyond the mindset that keeping the Sabbath holy means living right only on a designated day, whether it be a Saturday, a Sunday, or any other day of the week. This mentality is displayed, in particular, by those who come to church on holidays such as Easter, Thanksgiving, Christmas, and New Year's. They view their attendance on these days as a life changing experience or as if they are doing God a favor by gracing Him with their presence. God rebukes this shallow and meaningless form of reverence in **Amos 5:21** which states, *"I hate, I despise your feast days, and I do not savor your sacred assemblies."* The sacrifice that God desired was for them, as well as us today, to honor Him with our lives. God is not looking for part time employees. If I was in church right now, I would say, "Tell your neighbor, it's an everyday thing."

Let's not forget about those "Communion Sunday Christians." These parishioners misapply the importance of this church ordinance. Communion is a very sacred and vital part of our relationship with God; but communion alone, or the participation in it, will not save an individual. It is not a miracle fix-all. In fact, Holy Communion should serve as a reminder that Jesus gave His life for us, therefore inspiring us to give ours for Him.

Remember, He said, as often as you eat this bread and drink this cup, do it in remembrance. It is one more reason that we cannot live as though we are only saved for a day or on that day.

Even the great Mark Twain addressed this issue about "selective salvation" when he wrote, "Tom Sawyer pointed out a preacher that came to town who was so good that Huck Finn stayed saved until Tuesday." Though this was penned in a work of fiction, it holds true in reality, especially for the modern day Christian. We must get pass living or acting right on Sunday. Not to pick on Bro. Huck, but it must last past Tuesday.

The reason that some folk have this problem—living for Sunday—is because they get more engaged in the messenger than the message. The Apostle Paul attempts to shun this type of behavior in his letter to the Corinthian church. He says to them that his speech and preaching was not with persuasive words, but of the spirit and power which come from God. In order to live as if we are saved every day, we must rely on God's power and not our own or that of the messenger. If not, we will find that our saved, sanctified-and-filled-with-the-Holy-Ghost behavior will begin and end on Sunday.

Let's look at this closer and put it into an everyday perspective. We make grand gestures on a Sunday that we would not otherwise do because we think it is more significant. Our radio finds its way to a different station on Sunday. Instead of listening to our usual love ballad or heading bobbing tune, we find "Amazing Grace" as our song of choice. Even our normal communication, both word choice and pitch, seems to get cast aside on Sunday. It is traded in for a softer tone and a "God bless you" greeting. Not to mention, our style of dress becomes more modest and less revealing on Sunday—out with the splits, miniskirts, backless dresses and plunging neck lines in an effort to be more conservative and definitely more concealed. I understand reverencing God; however, your entire character and presentation thereof should not have to undergo such a drastic metamorphosis. If so, these combined changes in actions and speech point to a person that lives like they are **saved for a day**.

The inconsistency in our behavior is the thing that leads people to call us hypocrites. They see us acting one way on Sunday or at church; then, they see us acting a very different way outside of church and on every other day. Some of them will even tell us that we are not saved. Even though it may not be a fair assessment, they base their judgment of us on what we show them.

In **Ephesians 4:1**, Paul says, *"I therefore, the prisoner of the Lord, beseech you to walk worthy of the calling with which you were called."* In simple terms, he is begging us to live out our belief daily. What we have been taught should be manifested in the way we act. It is especially hard to convince the unsaved that you are saved when they cannot see a difference in the way they act and the way you do. Yes, it is important for us as Believers to understand appropriate time and place. However, it is more important for us to know that truly reverencing God has no particular time or place. It is imperative that we become more conscious of our conduct, our character and our conversation in all settings.

Herein is where the trouble lies. It is so easy to get caught up in the mood of the day or in a go-with-the-flow type attitude. We become seduced by our environment and surrender to its yearnings. While we do have the sincere desire to do what is right, we yield to the overriding power of our flesh. At that time, we do not consider the effect that our behavior will have on how we are viewed by others. Our only focus is on the temporary pleasure of our choice. This tunnel vision, once again, leaves us looking like we are only saved for a day. It gives ammunition to those who already look at us with an eye of skepticism. It brings condemnation, not only upon the individual that commits the ungodly act, but upon the entire Christian family. Whether we think it is fair or not, most times society judges us as a group rather than as an individual.

The shame and disgrace of our actions isn't so easily forgiven by man as it is by God. Therefore, the call to walk the straight and narrow path ultimately works for our benefit. We must understand that it is better to be correct than to have to be corrected. I know you are saying it is easy for you, who have the power of the pen, to write this. You are totally correct in what you are saying; nonetheless, be reminded that I am also accountable to the same standard that you are. Remember, I face all the same challenges that you do.

So, now the question that arises in the mind of most people is, how do we get beyond living saved for a day? How do I transform my Sunday mindset into a permanent way of life? If you listen carefully, I will clue you in; here it is: God wants the total you. He wants you to sellout, submit, and surrender to the Him totally.

Are you ready for that kind of commitment?

Chapter 2

This Is Hard!

The challenge to Quit Living for Sunday will force you to look at some ugly truths about yourself, about your attitude, and about your actions. When an honest assessment is made, we all will find that in some areas of our lives our Sunday demeanor is inconsistent with what is manifested in our weekly behavior. This reality gives credence to the necessity for the scripture **James 1:22**, which states, *"But be doers of the word, and not hearers only, deceiving yourselves."*

At this point, most people would say, "You know I am trying, but this is hard!"

Although I agree that successfully meeting this challenge is at times truly difficult, it is not impossible. We must remember that scripture we all like to quote, **Philippians 4:13**, *"I can do all things through Christ who strengthens me."*

Several precepts, when applied, will aid us in this endeavor. First, we must be sure that we receive the Word of God. This initial principle compels us to have a teachable spirit, ultimately reminding the Believer that it is not for us to dispute or reject the gospel, but that it is paramount that we embrace and obey truths. Application of scripture in our daily lives will be evident to all and beneficial to us. **Matthew 7:24** says, *"Therefore whoever hears these sayings of Mine, and does them, I will liken him to a wise man who built his house on a rock: and the rain descended, the floods came, and the winds blew and beat on that house, and it did not fall."*

But even now, even after great teaching and with the presence of such strong incentives as offered by Matthew, I know. *STILL*, it is hard. For most, it is easy to say "Amen" when hearing the sermon preached on Sunday. Such acceptance of His Word, which also encompasses His will, requires no real work. However, moving that acceptance outside of those four consecrated walls isn't always an easy transition.

We know this to be true. We must be real. The Word of God rarely ever coincides with our personal plans or pursuit of pleasure. Therein lies the rub. Our flesh causes friction because it craves things that only lead to trouble, which will soon thereafter cause us to call upon God for deliverance.

We desire Christ to assume the role as Savior of our lives, which means that He rescues us from danger. On the other hand, we dread His position as Lord of our lives, which means that He rules over us. Simply put, we want salvation, but we want it without all of the rules and restrictions. We want it on our terms. It's almost like saying, "Save me, but don't tell me what to do." Or, "Come when I call you, but stay out of my business until I do." I hate to burst your bubble, but you can't have one without the other. When you accept

Christ into your life, you accept Him as Lord and Savior, not Lord or Savior

God says, "If you love me, keep my commandments." As Christians, we know, or should know by what we have been taught, that it's the right thing to do, that we should follow the rules (i.e. The Golden Rule, The Ten Commandments). Yet, it's still hard!

So now you're asking yourself: How can I move from just being a hearer and become a doer? How can it become easier for me to make the transition? How can I Quit Living for Sunday?

The <u>second precept</u>, after receiving God's Word, is allowing it to permeate our thinking and inevitably alter our actions. **Romans 12:2** states, *"And do not be conformed to this world, but be ye transformed by the renewing of your mind, that you may prove what is that good and acceptable and perfect will of God."* If we are truthful with ourselves, we can admit that in some way, shape, or form we all are fashioned by a secular standard of living. It is hard not to be somewhat influenced by the alluring power of a mesmerizing world. Believers must begin the constant task of shedding worldly ideals in exchange for the spiritual conditioning provided by the Word. Plainly speaking, if we think right, we can act right.

That's why Philippians 4:8 tells us, *"Finally brethren, whatsoever things are true, whatsoever things are honest, whatsoever things are just, whatsoever things are pure, whatsoever things are lovely whatsoever things are of good report; if there be any virtue and if there be any praise, think on these things."*

True spiritual transformation always starts in the mind. A mind that is worldly controlled will be displayed through an unstable life, which is moved by culture. Whereas a mind that is shaped and directed by the Holy Spirit will enable us to act according to the Word of God and not by the whims of popular fads. This process of moving from being flesh controlled to being spirit controlled is called sanctification.

Sanctification is a progressive work. It begins at regeneration and operates in the hearts of men through the presence and power of the Holy Spirit. It is accomplished through the Word of God, with much prayer and self-examination. Lastly, the most important as well as most difficult step in sanctification is self-denial. Telling the flesh no is the same as telling a spoiled child they can't have an object they desire. You must prepare yourself for their tantrum and be willing not to give in just to change their reaction. Being steadfast is a necessary quality, for a Believer.

Again, it rings true; this is hard but not impossible. The Apostle Paul confirms this by stating in **Philippians 1:6**, *"Being confident of this very thing, that He who has begun a good work in you will complete it until the day of Jesus Christ."*

So, it would be safe for me to say, and you too, "I

am an unfinished product. Yes! I am a work in progress."

The reason we are motivated to engage in this never-ending process—to have a transformed mind—is because it will lead us to do what is good and "acceptable" in the eyes of God. It is only after the initiation of this everyday process that we can see ourselves progressing from "hearers only" to "doers of the Word".

I am no mind reader, but I know what you're thinking here because I thought it too. "Moving beyond being a hearer only just became harder and I'm only human."

Chapter 3

I'm Only Human!

"I'm Only Human!"

How many times have we heard this statement? Or, how many times have we been guilty of making it ourselves?

"I'm Only Human!"

Christians utter this phrase in an attempt to ease our conscience or even garner sympathy from other Believers. Nevertheless, we cannot hide from the fact that our human weakness, although always forgivable, is never excusable in the eyesight of God. **1 John 1:8-9** expresses explicit confirmation of this thought in writing, *"If we say that we have no sin, we deceive ourselves, and the truth is not in us. If we confess our sins, He is faithful and just to forgive us our sins and to cleanse us from all unrighteousness."* We can neither disguise our carnal desires nor compensate for them once acted upon by rendering the "I'm only human" excuse. Flimsy at best, it is merely a crutch that will not justify us when we stand before a righteous judge.

Yes, we are human. Yes, we do make mistakes. Verily, **Romans 3:23** states *"For all have sinned and* *fall short of the glory of God."* However, this has become one of, if not, the most overly used scriptures to validate Christians operating outside of the Word and Will of God. Yes, we transgress knowingly (by commission) or unknowingly (by omission), but this verse should never be taken out of context as a license to freely commit sin. This verse should be a continual reminder that we could never satisfy God's requirement for righteousness. Furthermore, it should point us to the importance of God's grace and the redemptive work that Jesus achieved on the cross. It should also humble us while creating in us a greater sense of gratitude for His atonement of our many sins.

The theological principle of salvation through grace alone alludes to a new dilemma. The problem which now arises is a misconception that continued sin would magnify God's grace in our lives. Sound spiritual doctrine exposes this fallacy, as so eloquently explained by the Apostle Paul in **Romans 6:1-2**, *"What shall we say then? Shall we continue in sin that grace may abound? Certainly not! How shall we who died to sin live any longer in it?"* We must be careful not to take on that "Oh-well-God-will-forgive-me-anyway" attitude. It should be our aim to live as sinless as possible.

Paul wrote from a familiarity that can only come from personal experience in struggling with our sinful nature. After all, it was him who penned in **Romans 7:15**, *"For what I am doing, I do not understand. For what I will to do, that I do not practice; but what I hate, that I do."* His admission can literally be paraphrased, "I am only human."

Paul had extensive knowledge of the Word of God. Also, like most Christians, he had a sincere desire to please God. Unfortunately, most of us fall woefully short because we adhere to the yearnings of our flesh. This internal battle between spirit and flesh mystifies humanity. This clash between two identities makes us wonder about our ability to do what is right. But, there is an antidote given to us in the scripture:

"I say then: Walk in the Spirit, and you shall not fulfill the lust of the flesh. For the flesh lusts against the Spirit and the Spirit against the flesh; and these are contrary to one another, so that you do not do the things that you wish." **Galatians 5:16-17**

These verses tell me that in order to consistently overcome those powerful, sinful urges that derive from my human nature I must constantly allow the power of the Holy Spirit, through faith, to lead me in controlling my actions.

I guess by now some of you are saying to yourself that I make it sound so easy! But, on the contrary, it's not easy. However, it is possible.

We never want to understate or minimize the damaging effect of the flesh when it is not under subjection. Its ugly head is reared in our poor choices and unseemly actions. Even though we are saved, we display worldly behaviors and habits, for which we self-pardon under the guideline of "I am only human."

Sometimes, we even say, "Well you know I have to do something" or "that's not that bad" or the real guilt reliever, "I am not hurting anyone." Which is such self-denial, we are hurting ourselves by the action and others by the example we set through committing the action.

So, what does God expect of me? Do I have to give up everything? We are given insight into what He expects of us in **1st Peter 4:1-2**, where he says, *"Therefore since Christ suffered for us in the flesh, arm yourselves also with the same mind, for he who has suffered in the flesh has ceased from sin, that he should no longer live the rest of his time in the flesh for the lust of men, but for the will of God."*

I know for some people this seems to validate the conclusion that you arrived at in the end of Chapter 1, which is, "It just got harder." You feel as though the very words, "has ceased from sin" and "doing the Will of God" seem to somehow disqualify you. Or, at the least, these measuring sticks are, often times, a stretch. I know, you are still saying, this is impossible.

Well, with God all things are possible.

Keep in mind the importance of your actions. In that same, fourth chapter of Peter, the Apostle also tries to help us to see the futility of our immoral actions. In verse 3, he proclaims, *"we have spent enough of our past lifetime in doing the will of the Gentiles, when we walked in lewdness, lusts, drunkenness, revelries, drinking parties, and abominable idolatries."* Basically, we have wasted enough time doing what is wrong.

Now, because we are a new creation in Christ, it is time to do what is right. We must move from living sinfully to attempting to live sinless. We must move from doing what we want to doing what God desires of us. In order to accomplish this seemingly impossible task, we have to follow the scripture and arm ourselves with the mind of Christ. Ultimately, Peter is saying, if I think Godly thoughts, it will produce Godly actions!

I know, I know, "You're only human," right? And, you have more questions. You are saying, "It sounds good in theory, but will it work for me?"

Chapter 4

Will It Work for Me?

The strange thing about any prescription, formula, solution, suggestion, or idea is the looming question, "Will it work for me?" Once applied, will I receive a positive result as a benefit of my hard work and sacrifice? Or else, why do it at all?

Let's be real. We are not as much concerned about what something did for someone else. We are more concerned about what we can expect to gain from it ourselves. Even after witnessing the undeniable evidence of success in the lives of others, we still have a tendency to question the effectiveness of whatever being applied as it relates to us. Subsequently, we either fail to do it all together or we only give a half-hearted effort. Sometimes our lack of effort is connected to our lack of expectation. Simply put, we don't believe it will work for us.

Never underestimate the power of believing. For example, look no further than sports. Even the once, often down casted, bag-wearing-fan who supported the New Orleans Saints had a song; it was also their motto: "I believe!" And, if a sports franchise can adopt this powerful concept of believing in themselves and their ability, why can't the Body of Christ believe that through Him all things are possible? Why can't we believe that His Word will do what it says it will do? Why can't we believe that we are overcomers and conquerors? Why can't we believe that if we submit to God and resist the devil he will flee from us?

The "Saints" of God should not invoke a doubtful spirit that questions, "Can it work for me?" but rather a boldness of attitude that says "Yes, it will work for me."

Sadly, we succumb to our own weaknesses and fears due to a lack of faith. This yielding is not limited to non-Christians or immature Christians but also includes mature Christians. We all like to quote that familiar scripture in **2 Timothy 1:7** *"For God has not given us a spirit of fear, but of power and of love and of a sound mind."* The uncomplicated truth is that fear is a by-product of a lack of faith. So even though God did not give us fear, the reality that it does exist is not changed. Not only does fear exist, but its paralyzing affect has nullified the would-be accomplishments of many people.

We read the Bible as if it is merely a book of stories for our personal entertainment; most agree that it is good reading. Others think it is filled with good suggestions. It is much more than that. It is the truth of God's Word. It is meant to bring us to faith in Jesus, so we may have life by believing in His name. This belief in His name is more than just a casual familiarity of who He is, but it also involves an intimate personal relationship with Him. This relationship is consummated when we learn to trust His will and obey

His voice. *"My sheep hear My voice, and I know them, and they follow Me. And I give them eternal life, and they shall never perish; neither shall anyone snatch them out of My hand."* **John 10:27-28.**

So when the question is asked, "Will it work for me?" In relation to the Word of God being an effective tool, it is really a question about deliverance. I find that I am an active participant, in my own personal deliverance. Someone is saying how is that possible? Well, the phrase "hear my voice" means it is our job to obey Him. The phrase "they follow me" means it is our job to trust Him. Our biggest problem is we become consumed by the fear of the outcome. Since we are unsure of how things will work out, we abandon the course of action presented in the scriptures and result to relying on our human instincts.

Consequently, all of those, "Yes Lords", and the many times we said, "Amen", on Sundays turn into a meaningless display. It's all cosmetic, a layer of paint that will soon peel. Now your worship seems like all looks and no substance. Effectively, you are living for Sunday.

Rather than falling into this unstable form of behavior, we should reflect on the biblical testimonies of our predecessors—our guide. For examples, let's look at two familiar episodes of deliverance through faith in the book of Daniel. <u>One</u>: The three Hebrew boys obeyed God by refusing to worship anyone else but Him. <u>Two:</u> Daniel displayed an identical, unwavering obedience to the Word of God; he prayed in spite of the king's decree outlawing prayer, which resulted in him literally being thrown to the lions. Each trusted the Lord, even in the face of a deadly fate. In both situations, we see how these faithful people were active participants in their own deliverance. Their level of commitment to God would not allow them to yield to the will of man. Not even at the risk of losing their own lives in a fiery furnace heated 7 times hotter or life and limb in a den of hungry lions

These two examples feature the most literal interpretation of **Mark 8:35** *"For whoever desires to save his life will lose it, but whoever loses his life for My sake and the gospel's will save it."* The application of these principles of obedience and faith doesn't always eliminate the presence of adversity, but it gives us hope in the very face of it. At the conclusion of both of these seemingly tragic events, we see the glory of the Lord manifested in the lives of those who obey and trust in His Word.

Figuratively speaking, we all have been there—in the fiery furnace or in the lion's den. Sadly speaking, many times we fall to the pressure of these experiences. We bow to the golden image. **James 1:14-15** states *"But each one is tempted when he is drawn away by his own desires and enticed. Then, when desire has conceived, it gives birth to sin; and sin, when it is full-grown, brings forth death."*

Yes, we do yield to the temptations. We give in. We sin. Then, we're left with a dismal and grave outlook: physical and/or spiritual death.

I guess you are saying, so what is the magic formula for this. How do I win in this no-win situation? Well, the reality is that there is no magic formula. Don't lose faith just yet. Never fear, the Bible is here. Again, the Word of God does provide us with a valid solution. **1 Corinthians 10:13** says *"No temptation has over-taken you except such as is common to man; but God is faithful, who will not allow you to be tempted beyond what you are able, but with the temptation will also make the way of escape, that you may be able to bear it."*

So, if you are still asking, "Will it work for me", it may be time to assess your consistency of obedience as well as your level of faith. I believe you will arrive at the conclusion that you can use some enhancement in both areas. In other words, if you want a different result, try a different course of action. Trust me, it works.

Chapter 5

Yeah, but When?

We've addressed that "This is Hard." We've acknowledged the "I'm Only Human" aspect and even dealt with our doubt of "Will It Work for Me." Okay, now we're getting somewhere, right? I know…"Finally!"

"Finally" is a term that deals with the "when." An important question weighing on everyone's mind, especially Believers, is "When?" It is also the basis of this chapter: "Yeah, but when?"

The answer to "When" is different for everyone. To return to those bag wearing Saints fans, their when (and win) was manifested after the franchise was in existence for 41years. That's when the team won its first, super bowl championship. But, imagine the numerous, doubtful moments that they experienced on their way to their ultimate destiny. Not only did frustration wreak havoc among the players in the locker room, but even more in the lives of the loyal fans.

I can envision one player having said to another, "Hang in there, our time will come." And, the teammate replying, "Yeah, but when?" I could even hear the loyal fan, who had been taunted by the opposition's question of "Yeah, but when?" resolutely saying, "Don't worry about us, we will win."

Well, the Saints did win. It came to fruition. Through faith, so will yours.

Even in the political spectrum, we see long awaited firsts make their way to the surface time after time. It occurred with the likes of President Abraham Lincoln and FDR, who after initial failures finally succeeded in achieving the highest office in the land. No doubt, these great men asked the question, "When? The most recent political example comes in the form of Barrack Obama, who is the first American President of color. As a country, it wasn't a question of "Yeah, but when?" For most, the thought of a non-Caucasian President was considered out of the realm of possibility.

Nevertheless, all of these, "Yeah, but when's" happened. Through faith, so will yours.

How many times have you asked yourself? "When? When will I…?" Right now, you're probably saying, "Yeah, but when… When will I receive the deliverance, the healing, the breakthrough, the prosperity, the relief, the peace, and all the other promises found in the Word of God? How long will I have to endure my present circumstances before I see a change?

In the **13th Psalm**, David asks the question, "How long?" four times in the first two verses in regards to his dilemma. It is not that he doubts in any way that God is hearing him or even whether God will respond. Yet his inaudible cry of, "Yeah, but when", can be heard. His anxiety is clearly revealed in this short but intense Psalm of lament. He seeks an answer, which is evidently eluding him at the time.

Like David, we too become frustrated when progress is slow or even absent. However, his very question, "How long," is evidence of delay but not of a final denial. There is a difference between the two; although in the mind of some people, they are one in the same. For them, the only clear line of distinction between delay and denial is fruition. Plainly speaking, they only know that there is a difference between the two once they receive what they have been asking for.

Know you're not alone. This type of Christian has always existed. We all fall into what the Bible describes as, "Oh ye of little faith."

We as church going folk like to use the cliché, "He may not come when you want Him to, but He's always on time!" Well, if we believe this to be true, just wait on Him! We must make a commitment to trust God, even when it seems like His watch is broken. Remember the timing of your salvation, in any situation, is not predicated on your personal fatigue. It is based on God's sovereign will.

I feel that the consensus among Believers is that, when we pray, God takes too long to get the message. Ironically, it is us who take too long to get the message. God will even use our trials to teach us how to totally depend on Him. It is amazing how the arrival of His mercy will be the turning point in moving us from despair to hope. There are so many biblical examples of God's powerful deliverance to aid us in learning to trust in the midst of despair. Still, the greatest ones are found in our own personal lives. There is no greater testimony than your own. Pass performance is the greatest antecedent to present trust.

There is an epidemic of spiritual amnesia in the church. We always seem to forget our previous victories while facing our present adversities. The memories of what He has done should increase our faith to trust Him for what He is about to do. In the midst of your last storm, you didn't know when God would show up, but He did. Along with His presence came His power; and through your deliverance, He got His glory.

The book of Judges records a powerful story reminiscent of the attitude we display during our times of struggle. Gideon gives voice to our inner turmoil, as we struggle with the issues of life. Even though we are people of faith, it is sometimes hard to remain faithful during crunch time. An angel of the Lord spoke to Gideon saying *"The Lord is with you."* Many times, we hear this from those around us during those stormy periods of our lives. And we reply just like Gideon did in **Judges 6:13** *"Gideon said to Him, O' my Lord, if the Lord is with us, why then has all this happened to us? And where are all His miracles which our fathers told us about."* Like Gideon, we are, in essence, saying, "Yeah but when?"

When we view a situation, we look at it with regards to our own personal weaknesses and our inability to rectify it. We must realize that the Will of God shall be accomplished not because of us, but in spite of us. Gideon looked at the number of his opponents rather than who was his ally. It is not how many you have on your team that assures you the victory; rather, it is who is on your team. We have the Lord on our side. We are His Saints.

God confirmed this for Gideon in **Judges 6:16** *"And the Lord said to him, surely I will be with you, and you shall defeat the Midianites as one man."* This is a reflection of the principle that you plus God are the majority. (You + God = Majority).

It is only when we become blinded by our own ineptitude that the "when" in our "Yeah, but when?" seems far and distant or even non-existent.

This chapter is not a condemnation of the level of your faith or even the existence of it, but an admission that we all fall short of fully trusting God sometimes. It is ironic how God will use the testing of our faith to help bolster our faith. That is why we should meet the question of "Yeah, but when?" with the scriptural responses, such as the one recorded in **Hebrews 11:1**. *"Now faith is the substance of things hoped for, the evidence of things not seen."*

This verse is not so much a definition of faith as it

is a description of what faith does. Faith is the proof that what cannot be seen does actually exist. The paralyzing grip of uncertainty can now be released by the positive expectancy of manifestation. We can stop concentrating on when it will come and move to an attitude of thankfulness that it will. There is no greater demonstration of faith than to praise God for something that can't even be seen yet.

It is at this point that even those around you begin to believe, because your faith is contagious!

Chapter 6

It's Contagious!

Normally, when we hear the phrase, "It's contagious", it is viewed negatively. We automatically think of something that we want to stay far away from. We assume it to be some life threatening disease. "I know I don't want what they have!" we exclaim! "This person should be quarantined! I may not be a genius, but I know the word contagious means caught by contact, or worse, airborne."

Well, that definition is correct; however, in this case, the interpretation is wrong. In this context, the person is infected. The only thing that he or she is infected with is great faith. This communicable element will not harm us, but move, motivate, and inspire us.

In light of this new information, we should be saying, "If they must be quarantined, you can put them in the room with me." We should be able to tell people I don't mind catching what they have. As a matter of fact, I wish I could rub against them so it would get all over me.

We must never underestimate the power of positive interaction. There is much to be said for the influence that we can have on others by the demonstration of our faith in action. Our faith is shared by others as they witness our conduct. It is shared when we testify to the works of God in our everyday lives. The Bible even gives weight to this in **Proverbs 27:17**, *"As iron sharpens iron, so a man sharpens the countenance of his friend."*

Subsequently, it seems imperative to me that my inner circle is comprised of people that live by faith. It would be to my demise to encompass myself with those who haven't learned to walk by faith and not by sight. The immature Christians in your life are meant to learn from you, whereas the mature Christians in your life are there for you to learn from them. The question arises: Which ones are you following?

We can't grow or advance by duplicating the actions of weak, timid, doubtful Believers. Everyone has encountered that person who is not moved by their circumstance but motivated by their tremendous faith. The more you are in their company, the more you find that their "I can, it will work out" attitude begins to rub off on you. That's because "It's contagious."

This "Can-do" quality is an especially important possession for those in leadership. It is hard to motivate a group of people to work toward a common goal when the leader doesn't even seem to believe it is attainable. This basic premise of "I can" is taught to children in their developmental years. A parent always tells a child don't say "You can't. Take that word—can't—out of your vocabulary." They are in essence teaching the child to believe in themselves and their ability to accomplish great things. Likewise, spiritually, God is our Heavenly Father, and He teaches us to believe in ourselves and in our ability to be successful by believing in Him and relying on His strength.

The proof is in the Bible. *"I can do all things through Christ who strengthens me."* What a powerful tool **Philippians 4:13** is in the hands of those who really apply it. The problem with this scripture, as with many, is that it makes for eye catching bumper stickers and great text material. It excites readers as a thought for the day, garners much attention as religious wrist bands. Alas, I am sad to report to you that it is extremely under used in practical application by countless church folks. Excessive quoting of scriptures does not count.

"It's contagious" shouldn't be a reference limited to what we say. It should be a mandate for how we live. Faith is more than a spoken word. It is a constant way of life. **Galatians 3:11** states *"The just shall live by faith."* This personal albeit public display will serve as a guide to those who are still struggling with trusting through tragedy.

At present, the issue becomes how do you handle the tough times? Do you wallow in self-pity and despair or do you remain hopeful even when it seems hopeless? A formula to help us in this endeavor is recorded in **James 1:2** *"My brethren, count it all joy when you fall into various trails, knowing that the testing of your faith produces patience."* This passage is confirmation that all Believers will face unpleasant challenges that God will use as tools of refinement for our faith. Yet, for some to rejoice during this time of difficulty is quite a stretch.

A smile induced by a smile during times of jubilation should not be confused as a true symbol of contagious faith. This contagiousness is comparable to yawning because someone else yawned. On the other hand, a smile which is inwardly incited through a confident demeanor, even while facing an uncertain outcome, can surely have a contagious effect on others. It makes you say to yourself, "Boy, if he can still smile with all that he is going through" or "if she hasn't given up in the midst of her gloomy situation, I know there is still hope for me." I told you earlier. Be careful who you hang around because this faith stuff is contagious. If you hang around long enough, it may even get in you.

Faith is so very vital to our existence that the Bible witnesses to its passing on as a legacy. The Apostle Paul speaks to this principle in **2nd Timothy 1:5**, *"When I call to remembrance the genuine faith that is in you, which dwelt first in your grandmother Lois and your mother Eunice, and I am persuaded is in you also."* This text tells us that the people who were instrumental in Timothy's upbringing demonstrated a life of faith before him. Therefore, it was contagious, and he caught it. In essence, he got it from his mama.

Most of us deal with some issues that are hereditary. That is why we must fill out a questionnaire at the doctor's office. They want to see what conditions have been passed on to us through our family. Most times these conditions are ones we would rather not have. But, spiritually speaking, we would and should gladly accept the passing on of a powerful faith in an almighty God.

Let me stick a pin here. You know we believe in saying, "That's what my mama said." Or, "Well that's what my grandma said," which is fine and dandy. I only hope they were saying what God said. After all, faith is saying what God says, and standing on it.

We humans have a habit of adapting the behaviors, beliefs, and even the fears of those closest to us. Sometimes for the good and at other times for the worst, we find ourselves being molded in their image. It lends truth to the statement, "We are the company we keep" and can be a setup for the ole adage, "Birds of a feather flock together." All of us have someone else's fingerprints on our lives. The great thing about it is that you have control over whose prints are left there. You have a say in who you will allow to remain in your life and most importantly, who you will allow to be the major contributor in your development.

Just the same, in our Christian lives, we should have a mentor—that person who makes an indelible imprint on our lives. Yes, God is the potter, and we are the clay. Our lives are in His hands to mold, to shape. Still, we can all use that Big Brother or Sister—a person of impeccable character, a person that demonstrates unshakeable faith.

Are you catching it yet? The symptoms are there. As I look at **Romans 1:8**, we get a mental picture of a contagious faith. *"First, I thank my God through Jesus Christ for you all, that your faith is spoken of throughout the whole world,"* wrote Paul to the Saints of God in Rome. My sincere belief is that the Bible was written to create contagious faith, a powerful unwavering faith that moves from one to another, not by osmosis but through the demonstration of its effectiveness in the lives of those who exercise it. My sincere belief is supported by **John 20:30-31**, *"And truly Jesus did many other signs in the presence of His disciples, which are not written in this book; but these are written that you may believe that Jesus is the Christ, the Son of God, and that believing you may have life in His name."*

Notice, the focus here is on believing. Believing can simply be translated as faith. I know. Once more, there goes those two words—"belief" and "faith"—from Paul, from John, and from me. Our faith is and/or should be contagious. We must have faith in Jesus, who makes all things possible, if we only believe.

Yeah, yeah I hear you saying it—the same rebuttal as always: "You make it sound so easy!" And, I even hear your other questions, "Really? That's all it takes? Just believe?"

You're not the only one who had trouble with belief. Even the Bible, where I always point you to throughout this book, is littered with everyday people who tussled with their belief and believing. A quintessential model is Thomas. Where do you think we get the phrase a "Doubting Thomas"? Jesus reappeared after his death, as He said He would, but Thomas did not believe that He was the Risen Savior. It was not until Thomas put his hands in the crucifixion wounds of Christ that his doubt was quelled. Thomas, through his actions, was saying just like me, you, and other church folk today, "Really? Just believe? This sounds too easy."

Chapter 7

You Make It Sound So Easy

I know we're taught that we should not use the word "hate." But, while we're on the subject of church folk, that's one thing I hate about them, they make everything sound so easy. Just pray and believe and have faith and everything falls in place.

1. What…You don't have problems?
2. You don't get stressed out sometimes?
3. You don't ever wonder why your life is the way it is?

I've been on both sides of this type of third degree. I've asked these questions. I've had to answer these questions. Here are my answers:

1. I do have problems.
2. I do get stressed out sometimes.
3. I do wonder why my life is this way.

So, I guess I wouldn't fit in your church. Well, I guess you would say that I don't have any faith…or at the least, not enough faith. On the contrary, I do. I just don't find it as easy as you sometimes think or make it seem.

During my biblical research, I found people just

like us who had spiritual battles that demanded the need for faith to overcome them. Many times, it didn't sound that easy. Even though they eventually succeeded, it was not due to a straight line from faith to fantastic finish. Rather, it was a faith improved on the way to their destiny. If not in the beginning, by the end, they understood *"The race is not to the swift, nor the battle to the strong, nor bread to the wise, nor riches to men of understanding, nor favor to men of skill, but time and chance happen to them all."* **Ecclesiastes 9:11**.

The ecclesiastical writer gives quickness, power, prudence, intelligence and expertise. Of course, this list is not exhaustive, but a cross sampling of characteristics which can make us attain or be victorious. No matter what they may be or how proficient we are in them, we learn that relying on our personal attributes won't always guarantee us personal gain or victory. So, since expected outcomes will not always be realized, we must depend on our faith in God to strengthen us for unexpected realities.

One of my favorite sayings is, "Keep it real." Throughout this book, I have done so. It is no different here. I will keep it real. I won't try to fool you as if it is so easy. I will remind you that, by faith, it is possible.

The songwriter must have had me in mind when he wrote the lyrics to the song, "I Don't Feel No Ways Tired", specifically, the chorus line, "Nobody told me that the road would be easy…" This phrase helps to confirm what, for me, is more than a mere suspicion that even Christian life has many challenges. In fact, at times, the life of a Believer is riddled with more adversity than that of a sinner.

"Hopeless," you say? Not at all! The song didn't stop with doom and gloom as its finale; rather, it elicits hope as its lasting theme. The part of the song that resonates with me the most is the end of that same chorus line, which says, "...I don't believe He brought me this far to leave me." This kind of hope makes even the most difficult things possible. You will be amazed at the seemingly insurmountable odds that you will overcome through the power of belief.

So, BELIEVE. You ask, "When?" The WHEN starts WHEN YOU BELIEVE!!!

But, it doesn't stop with belief alone. Faith must be followed with action, which is where it becomes more of a challenge. Jesus makes sure we understand that following Him will not be an easy experience, but a worthwhile endeavor. Listen at His words in **Luke 9:23**, *"If anyone desires to come after Me, let him deny himself, and take up his cross daily and follow Me."* The benefit of our relationship with Him is the free gift of eternal salvation. While there is no need that payment is rendered for salvation, a Christian life is accompanied by struggles, trials, and disappointments that we must endure.

In other words, Jesus does not hide things in the fine print for you to discover, after you have signed the contract. I am sure you have heard, "The devil is in the details." This expression means the offer made—usually one of those too-good-to-be-true deals—sounds and looks so attractive that it lures you in as a willing and eager participant. It is not until later, when you have become fully vested, that you uncover things that make honoring the agreement extremely difficult. By that point, backing out of the agreement will result in certain penalties for you.

Sounds a bit underhanded, doesn't it? That's because it is. I am glad God doesn't operate that way. Truth and integrity are His character traits. Again, Jesus lets you know up front what to expect on this tedious journey.

By now, we should be getting a clear visualization of why it isn't as easy for us as some church folk make it sound with their "just believe" advice. "So, why not?" you inquire, "Why isn't it that easy? Isn't that what God is supposed to do…make our lives easy?"

Perhaps, an answer can be found in the countless times we fail to exhibit those godly principles of truth and integrity. These principles, which can be achieved through obedience, must accompany our faith in order to be successful.

Faith is not a genie in the bottle. Nor, does it operate like the On-Demand feature from our cable provider. There's no "Push of a button" ease. We must exercise faith and obedience; and even then, it is so important for us to understand that we may not receive instant gratification and that there may not always seem to be a fair exchange.

The enemy frustrates the people of God by using our need for instant gratification against us. It is evident when we say things like, "Look, I have faith. I did things the Godly way. So where is my blessing? You told me it would work." The simple truths are: although you expect to, you may not always get back what you put in; and if you do, it may not happen instantaneously. These facts are actually blessings in disguise.

How can I say this? Well, it is predicated on how you define a blessing. An accurate and astute definition will help you to maintain your focus, even when it seems as if nothing is happening for you or things are not quite fair.

It would be easier to stand firm on this opinion if a material manifestation (Getting a new dress, a new car, a new house) is your only view of a blessing. Nonetheless, this viewpoint is tunnel vision in its worst form. It constitutes an incomplete definition of a blessing because there's a failure to see the greater good or the larger picture, which is due to the focus on a smaller and limited (tangible) target.

Whether you recognize it, you are truly blessed, and favor isn't fair. And, blessings and favor are inextricably linked to faith with obedience. Proof can be found in **Hebrews 11:6**, *"But without faith it is impossible to please Him, for he who comes to God must believe that He is, and that He is a rewarder of* *those who diligently seek Him."* This scripture shows the necessity of both components—faith and obedience. Ultimately, it shows that this is the path to your reward or blessing.

I can hear you chuckling inside, saying, "He is proving my point again. It's not always easy to have faith (believing), and it's surely not easy to be obedient."

True, true and true again! God has some requirements that are quite challenging, but did you also hear that there is an awesome reward in it for you. I told you earlier that God's character is far different from ours. He is so gracious toward us, which should compel us to heed His voice and comply with His Word. In fact, when we are tempted to do contrary to what He has commanded us, it is He Himself that gives us the strength needed to withstand the temptation.

Here comes a praise point! *"Blessed is the man who endures temptation; for when he has been approved, he will receive the crown of life which the Lord has promised to those who love Him."* **James 1:12.** This is not a reference to a material, temporal possession of this world but an eternal inheritance which does not fade. What more could we ask for? I hope all this is making it a little easier for you to "Quit Living for Sunday!"

I know it would be a lot less complicated if our time spent in church on Sunday would grant us automatic access to carefree living. I'll be the first to tell you that this is only wishful thinking. We must still deal with the woes of life as they avail themselves. The good news is now we have the comfort of knowing that we don't have to face these issues alone. Moreover, we have the reassurance that handling them properly is not in vain, but it gets God's attention, meets His approval, and invokes His blessings.

At this point, I hear that voice inside your head whispering, "I think I am getting it. Just keep talking." Well I'll make a deal with you. You keep reading and I'll keep talking.

I know I told you what I hate about church folk, Let me be clear. By no means am I trying to over simplify things. I just want you to know what it takes to please God.

Being honest with you, Christianity is not lived out within the four walls of the church. We go there to learn. We leave there to serve. That information should help you in your attempt to "Quit Living for Sunday."

If you're anything like me, that truth—We go there to learn; We leave there to serve—should be good to hear. It dispels the myth about church folk and Christians being one in the same. Christians are Christians. Why is this distinction necessary? Well, sometimes, the people who offend the most and who may be the worst hell-raisers are church folk. Christians have more problems with church folk than so called "sinners." After all, the nasty disposition displayed and negative behaviors exhibited by sinners are already expected. On the other hand, if church is attached to your name, you are expected to act differently. Sad to say, it is church folk that talk and treat Christians like they are anything but a child a God, and in particular, while at church.

Therefore, just like the term "church folk" is a definite misnomer, the idea about the church experience may not be what you think and/or what was described to you. Subsequently, I, and now maybe you too, have come to this conclusion: It is not what I expected.

Chapter 8

This Is Not What I Expected

What exactly did you expect? Many times we have pre-conceived notions about how things will be in a certain setting. In our minds, we have already envisioned the entire scene. We have even gone as far as living out the moments spent there in meticulous detail. We act as a master puppeteer controlling the speech, actions, and attitudes of the others who are present at our great minstrel show.

From the opening of the curtain until the final encore, we are in control. Therefore, everything will go according to plan. No need to worry about any mistakes. Everyone will cooperate with me and fulfill their duties as scripted. It will all be so easy.

Then, all of a sudden a string breaks or a leg falls off. Maybe the curtain won't open. "I was in control," we say to ourselves. "How could this happen to me? It was supposed to be all so simple…all so easy." This is not what I expected."

When it comes to church, we are no different. We have our own preconceived notions of how things will be. We have already figured out how the people will act and how the service will flow. From our time of arrival to our moment of departure, everything has already been anticipated. We have even pictured where we will sit and who will sit next to us.

Then, all of a sudden that string breaks: "Brother Thomas took *my* parking spot." Or, "Sister Brown didn't speak to me today." Next, the leg falls off: "Oh no! Someone is in *my* seat." Or, "Can you believe it? The choir didn't sing my favorite song. And please, don't get me started on Pastor. That sermon was so pitiful. I could have stayed home because this is not what I expected."

The real problem does not stem from the things that happened to you at church. Let's be real. It is the result of your expectancy meter pointing in the wrong direction before you even got to church. The needle is pointing toward those things that have no spiritual value. These distractions only cause us take your eyes off of Christ. Unfortunately, many times we become victimized by this—what I call the Peter Syndrome— and we find ourselves sinking.

When Peter stepped into the water, his meter was already pointed in the wrong direction. His uncertainty of the identity of Jesus was the first mistake he made. This indecision was compounded by his doubt of what Jesus could do. While facing the winds of adversity that blew upon him, Peter allowed them to have greater influence on him than the power of God that would ultimately deliver him.

I must ask, "What do you expect when you go to church? In what direction is your meter pointed when you step into the sanctuary?" If you have a clear and concise knowledge of what to expect, then you wouldn't allow yourself to be so easily entangled by those unexpected mishaps I alluded to earlier. Strings breaking and legs falling off are a part of every church and make their appearance known at every service. They manifest themselves through those you expect it from and, oddly enough, from those you would never have expected to behave that way.

It's amazing to me how we are inclined to overlook unseemly behavior from certain folk and take great offense to the same act when perpetrated by others. Let's be honest, there is the existence of prejudice, even in the church. This discrimination is not a reference to racial prejudice, but a person or parishioner specified prejudice. This biasness towards certain individuals is one of the subtle or not-so-subtle ways that the enemy makes his way into the church.

One of the most challenging duties of being a Pastor is not related to preaching; it is getting the people who are preached to, to get along with one another. Real brotherly love… in the agape sense. Nothing seems to demand more energy, prayer, and consistent consultation than the effort to harmonize the flock. Someone in the congregation is always at odds with someone else in the congregation.

The strange thing is that each person always makes him or herself the victim, stating how he or she "gets along with everybody," but "somebody" is always starting something with him or her. The real problem is that that person can't get along with anybody.

This cancer is the worst form. It does no harm to the body, yet it's so detrimental to the soul. Let me be more specific, such a sickness does no harm to the physical body, but it greatly damages the Body of Christ.

A quick moment of personal testimony; and, like all testimonies should be, this one is relevant as well as encouraging and edifying to the body. My wife was diagnosed, healed, and delivered from breast cancer. Before undergoing several bouts of radiation, she had to endure surgery and then the draining process of Chemo-therapy.

Fueled by self-righteousness and foolish pride, this cancerous, Pharisee mentality needs the same aggressive course of treatment. Some stuff has to be surgically removed or purged out. This case needs the Word of God, acting as the ultimate form of Chemo-therapy and radiation treatment, burning off the dross and producing a humbled heart.

Just as with physical cancer, some people catch it in the early stages, making it easier to treat. Sadly, other cases aren't diagnosed until the latter stages, if diagnosed at all; and, it leads to spiritual death. What's even more disappointing is that it is due to that individual's own denial of the existing symptoms.

These are the people who shockingly say, "That is not what I expected" when they begin to experience the repercussions of their repetitive, toxic behavior.

We are warned about this in **Proverbs 26:11**, *"As a dog returns to his own vomit, so a fool repeats his folly."* A fool can be defined as one who repeats the same action and expects a different result. If you keep sticking your hand in water, you can definitely expect it to keep coming out wet.

Don't get me wrong. I am not anti-expectation. Expectation is a good thing. There is a tail side to this coin. I've told you what not to expect. Let me tell you what you should be expecting.

When you go to church, you can expect to be healed, because the Word of God has healing power. You can expect to be delivered, because the Word of God is liberating. You can expect to be changed, because the Word of God is life changing. We must expect not to leave the same way we came.

We have to do just like the lame man that is referenced in the third chapter of the book of Acts. In verse five, it says, *"So, he gave them his full attention, expecting to receive something from them."* When we come to church, God has to have our full attention if we expect to receive something.

One of the most disheartening things to a pastor is for people to come to church and leave the same way they came. There is a blessing in store for them, but they miss out on it because they allow themselves to become distracted. It reminds me of the tragedy of Martha in the gospel of Luke. She was in the very presence of Jesus, but missed the benefit of his teaching. Martha became distracted. She was so busy concentrating on what her sister Mary wasn't doing that she failed to do what would have blessed her most. The scripture says, *"Mary,"* however, *"sat at Jesus feet and heard His word."*

We have that same tragedy being played out in the church today. Many folk, while being in the house, miss the Word, because they worry about what someone else is or isn't doing. Jesus even pointed this out when He said, *"Martha, Martha you are worried and troubled about many things."* Martha had allowed herself to become irritated about something that was not her business. Martha was probably saying this is not what I expected. I am doing all the work, while she is sitting around. Martha had a distorted view of what being with Jesus was all about.

In this loving reprimand, Jesus told Martha that Mary had chosen the good part. This reproof let Martha, as well as us, know that nothing is more important than the Word. Unfortunately, many Believers today are just like Martha. They believe the more they rush around being busy, the more impressed the Lord will be with them. They spend many hours in church, yet fail to get the good part. In order to truly get what you need from the service, you have to have a clear understanding. You must ask yourself, what did you go there for?

Chapter 9

"What Did You Go There For?"

The greatest chance for success in anything is tied to understanding the purpose for which it is done. It is hard to be joyful about something that seems to be void of purpose. This is true in all aspects of life. Whether it is a job, a relationship, or some other endeavor, we need a reason to continue our involvement in it. This concept is even true of the church.

In the previous chapter, we talked about expectancy, as it relates to worship. Our main focus was on what we did not expect. However, we also know that there are many that attend service who do expect something great. These are the ones who aren't easily distracted because they know what they went there for.

We must be laser focused. It's like a trip to Burger King. We can't stuff ourselves with the fries; then have no room for the Whopper. After all, Burger King is known for their tasty, flamed broiled Whopper Sandwich. Similarly, too many church folk stuff themselves with the fries (distractions) and have no room for the Whopper (the Word). Believers know that the fries are the side while the Whopper is the main course.

My question is: **What did you go there for?**

"Therefore lay aside all filthiness and overflow of wickedness, and receive with meekness the implanted word, which is able to save your souls." **James 1:21**. This directive assures us of the benefit of staying focused on our purpose for going to church. Our true purpose for being there is played out in the words of a popular song by the group Mary, Mary. "Go get your blessing." Many people go to church looking for a blessing while failing to realize that the Word of God is your greatest blessing. It leads us to a greater understanding of what we can expect as a follower of Jesus Christ.

The Word of God is so precious that the psalmist says he will hide it in his heart that he may not sin against God. It shows his understanding of obedience to God's Word. And, obedience is better than sacrifice.

Just a few days ago, I visited a fine restaurant. The waitress recommended some appetizers and I refused. I did not want to get filled up and then not be able to enjoy or have room for my main course. I knew what I went there for and wouldn't allow anything to keep me from getting it. I'm sure you can relate. Many of you have been guilty of that. The entrée became a part of your doggie bag. Regrettably, when you bring it home and warm it up the next day, it does not always taste as good as when it was fresh and hot.

This same principle can apply to church. When it's

time for the Word of God to go forth, our attention span has met its quota. Therefore, we miss the best part, which is the sermon. It is equivalent to throwing away the Word. Again, the question arises, "What did you go there for."

I don't need too many appetizers. No carry-out-plate of cold leftovers that will probably get thrown away! I want to get that preached gospel, freshly anointed. It is paramount.

The Word of God should not be treated merely as a book of suggestions but as a precious wealth of life-giving knowledge. Since it gives us the remedy we need to successfully overcome our daily struggles, we should treasure it. Not only does it give us **B**asic **I**nstruction **B**efore **L**eaving **E**arth, it gives us hope.

We can rely on God's Word as a competent source of guidance. This vital tool is useful in teaching us the way to eternal salvation, and moreover, serves as reassurance of God's presence in our daily salvation. Therefore, my primary reason for going to church is to get the Word. It hearkens back to a verse from one of my favorite songs, "In Times like These." This song says, "In times like these, we need the Bible." Yes, I fully agree that the unadulterated gospel is what we need in times like these.

The 13th chapter of the book of Matthew presents a parable of the sower. In its presentation, we find four types of attitudes in receiving God's Word. Three of them demonstrate a poor but yet prevalent response to the Word of God. It shows that there is a lack of understanding of the true benefit that we can obtain through properly applying scripture to our daily living.

Sadly enough, many lifelong Christians fall into these unfortunate categories. When we look at the fourth and final one of these types, we gain insight into the great value of a positive attitude toward His Word. **Matthew 13:23** says, *"But he who received seed on the good ground is he who hears the word and understands it, who indeed bears fruit and produces: some a hundredfold, some sixty, some thirty."* This category represents those people that know what they went there for and refuse to leave without it. This should be the attitude that every Believer should aspire to possess.

A popular phrase of today is, "I have to get a Word!" Usually, it is preceded by or followed with, "I don't have time to play." This statement is so powerful and very truthful, because we really don't have time to waste. However, many of the people that make this profound declaration fail to utilize the Word of God to their benefit. It is good enough for them to shout on, but not good enough for them to stand on.

We must realize that the Word is a firm foundation. Its reliability has been proven down through the generations. **John 17:17** bears out its immutability. *"Sanctify them by Your truth, Your Word is truth."*

True appreciation for the Word of God comes with

maturity. The Apostle Paul says in **1ˢᵗ Corinthians 2:6**, *"However we speak wisdom among those who are mature,"* As I see it, wisdom can be defined as the application of knowledge. Therefore, the claim to be wise, which is made by way too many, seems to be futile. Perhaps they have learned how to quote the Word of God, but they fail miserably when it comes to living it. It becomes wasted time, if you go to church to get the Word, and leave it in storage when you need it. Simply put, the Word only works if you work the Word.

"Just Do It" should not only be the Nike slogan. "Just Do It" should be a Believer's way of life as it relates to the Word of God. We shouldn't try to rationalize it. We must be convinced of its viability.

We can get help in this area from **Isaiah 55:11**, which states: *"So shall My word be that goes forth from My mouth; It shall not return to me void, But it shall accomplish what I please, And it shall prosper in the thing for which I sent it."* God gives us His personal guarantee that the preached Word is not for entertainment purposes. The preached Word should be viewed as a master tool in the hand of a skillful worker. Know that the key to your success comes in properly using the tool and not from just holding it. This application is the only way to get good results. See you can walk around with a bible in your hand all day long, however, if you never read it, never understand it, and most of all, never apply it, you might as well discard it in the nearest trash can because it is of no value to you.

Now I hear you repeating your question from an earlier chapter of this book. You are saying to yourself, "Although he makes it sound so easy, I still wonder will it work for me?"

The best way to make a believer out of you is to allow you to make a believer out of yourself. All I can say is try it, you might like it.

Chapter 10

Try It; You Might Like It

One of the most dangerous and also most undetected attitudes in the church is that of complacency. We are so accustomed to doing things a certain way and expecting certain results. We are so programmed in our actions and robotic in our mannerisms. We have achieved a certain level of comfort and do not want to extend ourselves beyond that zone. We fail to go the extra mile in our ministry, in our praise, and especially in our obedience to the Word of God, which is the most important.

We know when to clap, praise, stand, shout, wave, and witness. Saying "Amen" comes naturally at designated points in the service. In other words, we have this "church thing" down to a science. We leave with that familiar phrase dripping from our lips: "Church was good today." Unfortunately, all too often, this statement is more of a description of the mood of the service rather than the benefit extracted from being an active participant in the service.

Before you get angry with me, please allow me to share my point of view with you. I do not doubt the quality of your worship service, nor do I question your personal enjoyment of it. Nevertheless, my greatest desire is that we take full advantage of the service and ultimately of what we went there to get, which is the Word. I want our attendance to be a life changing experience. And the only way this can happen is if we leave with a Word that we can apply to our everyday life.

Please know that we have all been guilty of leaving the Word at church. The challenge for us is to bring it home; bring it to work; bring it to the communities we live in; bring it to neighbors, friends, love ones, and most of all, bring it to the lost. One of the greatest ways to do this is by allowing them to see it alive in our own lives.

This task takes hard work and constant reinforcement on our part. Yet, the tremendous gain is worth all the sacrifice! So try it; you might like it!

Many of us have spent countless years in church before coming to the realization that we were doing it, mostly, as a social activity or as an expected behavior. Some people still cannot bring themselves to admit this ugly truth. In the 2nd chapter of this book, I warned you that we would have to face some ugly truths about ourselves. This is one of them.

Another harsh reality is that we went to church out of a sense of obligation instead of personal commitment. Many times, we did it in an effort to please a nagging love one or to give a certain impression to those we respect. Even when our attendance was self-prompted, it was motivated by the person to person fellowship rather than a sincere effort to build a more Christ centered relationship. Sunday, so to speak, was a day we knew we would surely see our friends and have an opportunity to fellowship with them.

We must face, accept, and correct our behavior to inevitably change for the better, beginning with a change in our attitude and mindset. I hope by now you have come to realize that this fellowship is great, but relationship is the greater reason for going to church.

Yes, **Psalm 133:1** says *"Behold, how good and pleasant it is for brethren to dwell together in unity!"* However, the mark of mature Christians is that they place more value on God's Word than on being popular with God's people. Many times, in the attempt to be a people pleaser, we will find that we aren't pleasing God. Through spiritual growth, we can learn how to let the Word of God become the centerpiece of the worship experience. After all, Believers go get it, leave with it, and live by it.

Once again, it is because of spiritual growth that mature Christians have come to understand how important God's Word is in day-to-day life. "What would Jesus do" is more than just a slogan on a wrist band, keychain, or bumper sticker. It becomes a constant rhetorical question that leads to a wise answer. It forces them to take the moral high ground in situations that would usually lead to a dishonorable outcome.

Now the Word becomes an invisible spiritual

ladder that helps mature Christians climb above the negative attacks of the enemy. It becomes their means of exaltation. It helps them to stay focused on the mountain, even while they are in the valley. It gives them hope in the face of hopelessness. It gives them strength, even in their greatest time of weakness. Now, instead of becoming the victim, they become the victor. A new creature has been created. A life has been transformed, through the power of the Word.

This transformational element is the reason why I told you, "Try it, you might like!" It is because God's Word has a proven track record of success, as evidenced in the scripture. It is not just good advice. It is not someone's personal opinion. It is not another good idea. It is not a simple suggestion. It is a life changing prescription.

Moreover, the scripture is His commandments for us. **Deuteronomy 12:26-27** states, *"Behold, I set before you today a blessing and a curse: the blessing if you obey the commandments of the Lord your God which I command you today."* I may not possess genius level intelligence, but I do know the best choice to make.

Likewise, I do know that God does not impose His Word upon us. Subsequently, God has given us the right of choice. But, we must understand that along with the right of choice comes consequence.

We can choose to live like the world, which requires little or no effort and hardly any sacrifice. It does not reap a good reward either. On the other hand, Christian living requires both great effort and much sacrifice. It reaps both earthly and eternal rewards. I would rather choose the latter. How about you? Try it; you might like it!

In order to do this, live as a Christian, we must move out of our comfort zone. We must go beyond church as usual. We must shake off the spirit of complacency, which undeniably exist in the church. We must see the Word of God from a new perspective. It can no longer be seen as just the message that pastor preached last Sunday. Our vantage point must be that the gospel is a wealth of knowledge to live by from Monday to Sunday.

After all, the point of this book is to move you beyond living as if you are saved for a day, to get you to Quit Living for Sunday, remember?

"And I will give you shepherds according to My heart, who will feed you with knowledge and understanding." states **Jeremiah 3:15**. When someone feeds you something, you have to try it. Knowledge and understanding is a strange diet for some folk. It is not readily accepted because they really did not go there for that. It does not agree with their taste buds. However, what may not taste good to you may be good for you.

Too many people have a flawed understanding of the role of a pastor. They think it is his job to please their palates, or in essence, make them feel comfortable. When in actuality, it is the pastor's job to make them feel uncomfortable. When your sinfulness is not addressed, you will continue in it. Why should you change positions if you are already comfortable?

When you are confronted with your sins, it makes you feel uncomfortable. This "facing the mirror" is a necessary process in order for change to take place. It is why God charges the pastor to feed you knowledge and help you to gain understanding or a deeper insight. A wise man said of the shepherd (pastor), "It is his job to feed and lead. It is the job of the flock to swallow and follow." Ultimately, this quote highlights the fact that the pastor is only giving to you what God has given to him for you.

The pastor's preaching is designed to make you better and not bitter. **2nd Timothy 3:16-17** states, *"All Scripture is given by inspiration of God, and is profitable for doctrine, for reproof, for correction, for instruction in righteousness, that the man of God may be complete, thoroughly equipped for every good work."* These verses mean that God took an active role in revealing truth to the authors of His Word. They also remind us of the spiritual benefit we gain from following it properly. In addition, they show us the direct contrast between knowing God's Word and living God's Word. It is good to know but even better to do.

The blessing doesn't come from knowledge. The blessing comes from practical application. Touch your neighbor and say, "Nike!" Why "Nike?" Well, it's because we should "Just Do It."

    I know someone is saying, "Just do it would be good if we were machines. Then we could easily be programmed." Well, true, it would be easier if we were mechanical. Righteous behavior would then be commonplace and would require no thought or real effort on our behalf. In fact, it would be an automatic reaction to a designated situation. However, while being repetitious, this mechanical mind would not lend itself to the human emotions that drive us and separate us from any other creature or creation on earth.

    Our responses do differ, from time to time. At certain periods, we find ourselves in a different place emotionally. So to keep it real, even when we know the right thing to do, there are times that we just don't do it because we just don't feel like it.

Chapter 11

"I Just Don't Feel Like!"

Lack of knowledge is not the only barrier that keeps us from doing what is right. In fact, some of the most knowledgeable people seem to make some of the worst choices. Lack of knowledge is not the problem, but the lack of self-control is. Part of the reprimand that they receive from others includes the phrase, "Now you know better than that." Usually, this stern rebuke is followed by the question, "Why did you do that?" But before we interrogate them any further, let us consider our own bad choices.

"Therefore you are inexcusable, o man, whoever judge another you condemn yourself; for you who judge practice the same things." **Romans 2:1.** This verse is a wake-up call for the self-righteous. Beyond being a "mind-your-own-business" type of reminder that is needed by us all from time to time, it is a caution to never forget that we must sweep around our own front door before we try to sweep around others.

Speaking from personal experience, I have made my own share of bad choices. Not all of these were done out of ignorance, but rather from a selfish will. Sometimes we have all the information needed to make a wise choice; we just don't feel like it. I have told you numerous times, righteous living calls for personal commitment as well as personal sacrifice.

To be honest with you, there were and still are moments I just don't feel like it. I believe that, at certain times, we all find ourselves in this state of mind where we are moved by our feelings. However, faith over feelings is the best formula for believers to follow.

Our faith is the foundation of our value system. It is there that we derive a sense of right and wrong. It is the guide by which we live. However, we can still get caught up in inappropriate situations. This is not always due to lack of guidance; sometimes it's simply due to a lack of desire. In other words, we knew what was right, but we just didn't do it.

How does this approach to life differ from that of the non-believer? This conscientious choice to do wrong is a true contradiction to all that we stand for. It says I can do what I want, when I want and how I want. This attitude shows no sense of accountability. This selfishness lacks self-discipline. We are called to rise above this quicksand behavior. To step in it will surely cause us to sink.

It would be in our best interest to hear what God has to say about this matter. We can find this information in **1st Peter 1:15-16**. *"But as he who called you is holy, you also be holy in all your conduct, because it is written, 'Be holy, for I am holy.'"* The key part of this phrase is "in all." We cannot become satisfied with conducting ourselves properly only when we feel like it or in the situations that we choose.

Isn't it amazing that the watchful eye of others always seem to catch us at the most inconvenient times. The times that we allow ourselves to be flesh controlled is when we gain the largest audience. These spectators can't wait for the opportunity to say, "I told you so."

I know some of you are saying, "What is the big deal? Who cares what others think?" If you are one of those people, it shows that you really don't understand the overwhelming impact of your selfish behavior. It is so serious that the Apostle Peter felt the need to address it. **1st Peter 2:11-12** says, *"Beloved, I beg you as sojourners and pilgrims, abstain from fleshly lusts which war against the soul, having your conduct honorable among the gentiles, that when they speak against you as evildoers, they may, by your good works which they observe, glorify God in the day of visitation."*

As Believers, we are called to withdraw from behaviors that are self-indulgent but also self-destructive. We cannot allow the enticement of sin to be stronger than the resistance to sin. It goes back to the concept of, "Just Say No." In order to bring our flesh under subjection, we must learn to tell it no. It is foolish for Christians to give the flesh everything it craves.

I know it's hard, especially if you aren't used to doing it. But, the word is NO! Practice it, in order to perfect it. NO!

Even now, I can still hear you saying, "But I don't feel like it." And if you would indulge me for a moment, I would like to tell you what is also probably running through the minds of many of you. "I thought the Bible said whom the Lord has freed is free indeed. Well if this is true, why does Christianity seem to be so restrictive?"

I won't answer you with my opinion. What I will do is direct you to the answer in God's Word. **Galatians 5:13** states, *"For you, brethren, have been called to liberty; only do not use liberty as an opportunity for the flesh, but through love serve one another."* If you allow me to paraphrase, this scripture is saying you cannot do what you want to do. Liberty does not give one free reign. With liberty, comes responsibility.

You must understand that no one feels like doing what is right all the time. Nonetheless, the price for doing wrong is much higher than we realize.

There was a commercial that aired years ago saying, "Pay me now or pay me later." It was in reference to auto repairs. Payment now would be less expensive. The price of waiting, however, would be more costly due to the greater damage. Ironically, in this situation, we would have to pay now and later. The latter being the more costly.

Bad choices always cost us something. So, why do we even do it?

This dilemma is shared by the entire Christian community. None of us, not today or in biblical times, are exempt from this intense struggle. It is reflected in **Romans 7:15** *"For what I am doing, I do not understand. For what I will to do, that I do not practice; but what I hate, that I do."* The Apostle Paul is being honest about the fact that he does not even understand himself at times. He lets us know that there is a constant internal struggle between the spirit and the flesh. That the flesh, this powerful and often times overriding force, is what causes us to say I just don't feel like it. In essence, Paul is saying, "Even when I know right, I still do wrong because I felt like it.

When we read this text, we hear the sound of a man who feels defeated. Like us, he is an individual who appears to be powerless to sin. It can be heard in his voice. Paul even goes as far as calling himself a "wretched man." He points to his own sense of misery and distress.

His condition is a state that Believers find themselves in too. It is the result of not living according to the power of the spirit, but being driven by their fleshly desires. Paul subsequently poses a question out of his desperation. He asks, "Who will deliver me?" A question to which there is only one sufficient answer. We can only count on Jesus Christ, our Lord, to deliver us.

Even with the good news of deliverance from our own entrapment through sin, we must still deal with our lack of desire to do the right thing. We provide the enemy with strong evidence for an indictment against us. Please be advised that it is our conduct that shows people who we truly are at our core.

Dedication to proper behavior is imperative in a Christian life. John the Revelator speaks on this matter in **1st John 3:10**. *"In this the children of God and the children of the devil are manifest: Whoever does not practice righteousness is not of God; nor is he who does not love his brother."* This verse should serve as an incentive to do right even when we don't feel like it. To some people, this failure to do so not only denies the presence of God in our lives but also His power at work through our lives.

On the contrary, the manifestation of good behavior leads one to the belief that God's presence is a dominant force in our life. Needless to say, apart from God, we are powerless to do what is right. For confirmation of this matter, let us look at **1st John 2:29** *"If you know that He is righteous, you know that everyone who practices righteousness is born of Him."*

As truthful as we know and believe this to be, we still find ourselves falling short in this area. Therefore, we must strive harder day by day not to allow ourselves to be victimized by this spirit of complacency and self-indulgence.

It will take a great effort on our part to fulfill the plea we verbalize in our daily prayer when we say, "Let Thy will be done." It is imperative that every Believer put forth a diligent effort at becoming fully committed.

Chapter 12

Fully Committed

As we look at this phrase, "Fully committed," we know that it calls for a person to be thorough in their pursuit. We must be focused. We must be totally sold out. Wavering is not an option. Flimsy excuses cannot become the basis for inappropriate and ungodly actions. Not only must we decide to hold out, we must also be sold out.

To hold out means to withstand the yearnings of our flesh, no matter how strong the cravings become. We must deny, deny, deny! To sellout means giving in completely to the Will of God. Successful Christian living calls for total submission.

James 4:7 says, *"Therefore submit to God. Resist the devil and he will flee from you."* I find it strange that most people who quote this scripture fail to state the most important part, which is the first directive: the first directive: submission to God. It shows our responsibility.

We must be willing to resist wrongdoing. My brothers and sisters, this is not a Sunday thing. It is a lifetime commitment. Fully committed means standing up for what is right regardless of the circumstances or the environment. Unsure of its origin, I heard this statement that stuck with me.

"Right is still right even if no one does it; and wrong is still wrong, even if everyone does it."

These wise words reaffirm the fact that we must be fully committed in order to do what is right consistently. Many of us profess to have this type of resilience, until we are confronted with difficult situations. There's a difference between speaking up and standing up—bold speech minus the action to back it up. We all do right not to confuse the two.

Peter, known as the "spokesperson" among the disciples, was called Big Mouth Peter by some theologians since he had no problem speaking up. Yet, there were times that he had problems standing up. Let us look once more to one of the premier biblical examples involving him, when he was called out of the boat by Jesus and allowed to walk on the water. His mouth got him in the water, but his lack of commitment had him going under the water.

We can further examine Peter's life, as it relates to us, and find a greater example of his talking the talk but failing to walk the walk in **Matthew 26:35**. *"Peter said to Him, Even if I have to die with you, I will not deny you. And so said all the disciples!"* This was his way of saying that he was fully committed. I don't know about you, but Peter's claim of death over dishonor is full commitment. You cannot get any more committed than that. Nevertheless, it was only talk because in verses 69-74 of the same chapter, Peter denied knowing Jesus three times. He was more concerned about the consequences of owning up to his relationship with Jesus. Peter was worried about the personal inconvenience of being truthful. Instead of walking the walk, he walked away and wept bitterly. The one who spoke full commitment failed miserably when it came time to live it.

Peter's actions, as well as his reaction, did not surprise Jesus. This lack of true, full commitment had already been predicted by Jesus himself in an earlier setting. Before we judge Peter, remember, we too have been there and done that. Like him, we have been brash in our declaration and have fallen woefully short in our presentation. We have "talked a lot of noise" and failed to follow through.

We sing songs such as, "Fully Committed", "I Won't Turn Back", and "Sold Out." But, are we? How far are we willing to go for the cause of Christ? Are we only willing to speak up? Or, are we willing to stand up for Jesus Christ?

We take clichéd phrases and make empty promises. Does this sound familiar? "I am on the battlefield for my Lord. And, I promise Him that I will serve Him until I die." But do we really mean it? God knows our heart, our motives, and our intentions. All of these may be hidden from man; they are certainly transparent to our Omniscient, Omnipotent, and Omnipresent God. He knows that, at times, we don't even want to serve Him, yet alone die for Him. I often say, "He died for us, and we won't even live for Him." What does that say about our level of commitment?

From pulpit to pews, the universal church suffers from the lack of fully committed people. Those who hold leadership positions in the church seem to have the worst case of this strange ailment. There is no pill, shot, or cream to alleviate the symptoms or cure this disease. There is no quick fix or simple solution to get through it or to get over it. In order to be fully committed, you must be determined, focused, and faithful.

Let us look at the Apostle Paul's instruction on commitment. Directed to a young Timothy, they are helpful to us today. **2nd Timothy 2:1-3** states, *"You therefore, my son, be strong in the grace that is in Christ Jesus. And the things that you have heard from me among many witnesses, commit these to faithful men who will be able to teach others also. You therefore must endure hardship as a good soldier of Jesus Christ."*

Paul was in effect telling his son Timothy that we are engaged in spiritual warfare. He wanted him to know that being fully committed would be costly. He used the phrase "endure hardship" to speak to the severity of this challenge. While pointing out that which seems obvious to us, he also gives hope by letting us know that we are not dependent upon our own power to succeed.

I believe we can all say "Amen" to that because

there are times when all of us have found our strength to be insufficient.

We find that the strength to endure can only come from God. Again, He is the only correct answer and sufficient source.

Timothy is encouraged to pass on this powerful, liberating, and encouraging information to others. We build a strong Christian Community by passing the Word of God from one to another. As said in an earlier chapter, "It's contagious." We strengthen each other by our testimony.

After all, God did not intend for us to be selfish but selfless. It is implored through the scripture. **Psalms 78: 2-4** states, *"I will open my mouth in a parable; I will utter dark sayings of old, which we have heard and known, and our fathers have told us. We will not hide them from their children, telling to the generation to come the praises of the Lord, and His strength and His wonderful works that He has done."*

Just as in physical warfare, you need someone to cover your back, so is it in spiritual warfare. Although being fully committed is an individual attitude and decision, it takes a joint effort. Simply put, a little encouragement goes a long way. You would be surprised at the impact that your words can have on another Believer when they may be feeling a bit weak or vulnerable. This is what necessitates the presence of positive, motivating, and righteous-living people in our lives. We all need someone that can give us a Word when we need a boost. This statement is confirmed by **1st Thessalonians 5:11** *"Therefore comfort each other and edify one another, just as you also are doing."*

The reason for me addressing the issue of full commitment in the church is because we see the devastating effect of unfaithfulness on the local assemblies. It is evident in rehearsals, in meetings, in functions, in tithing, in Sunday Service, and, most importantly, in our everyday lives. We will quickly shun our responsibilities to our ministry in order to fulfill some secular or personal obligation.

Sometimes, it is unavoidable due to the circumstances of life. Other times, it is not. For example, when Believers are present physically in church, but their minds are still not focused on church. We have a way of being controlled as well as consumed by worldly projects and ultimately more committed to them. We have become more committed to social and secular clubs and organizations than we are to the things of God. We will not miss a little league game, soccer practice, Girl Scout meeting, bowling night, fundraiser, club party, band booster meeting, etc. We will bring donations, pay dues, and commit our time and energy doing whatever it takes to fulfill our commitment, even going as far as to rearrange schedules or take time off from work to be present. Imagine how effective the church could and would be if we showed that same level of commitment.

The only way for us to be truly committed to doing

the Will of God is by knowing the Word of God. We cannot do what He wants if we do not know what He says. God expects something out of us that we are not, and seldom feel like, giving Him. He wants our total self. As the song said, "He wants it all."

We do a good job of faking it on Sunday in order to win the praises of men, but what happens when Monday gets here? Our commitment is not measured by how loud we witness in church on one day out of the week. Not by the pleasant church demeanor we show while in God's house. Not by our award winning smile, by our beautiful garments, and not by our sanctimonious presentation. In fact, our commitment is not a "while I am at church" thing. Being fully committed is the thing that the Word of God teaches us how to be while we are in the world.

The Apostle Paul does not give us a definition of commitment. Rather, he shows us an example of a committed life. He says to us in **Philippians 1:21** *"For me to live is Christ, and to die is gain."* He knew his continued living would bring glory to God and further the cause of Christianity. He also understood that his death would bring him into the very presence of the One he had been living for and preaching about all that time.

Another very telling statement that fell from Paul's lips was that Christ would be magnified in his body, by life or by death. These words have a powerful impact. They were written by the Apostle while he was in prison and possibly facing death. It doesn't get more committed than that—the sacrifice of life.

In **2nd Corinthians 11:23-33**, Paul gives us an extensive list of all the problems and difficulties he faced for following Christ. He wants us to understand that commitment to God brings its own set of challenges. Sometimes, these challenges can be difficult and even overwhelming.

As a Believer, we cannot allow ourselves to succumb to the notion that being in a committed relationship with God will be a thing of convenience. The truth of the matter is that following God brings on inconvenience. The Apostle Paul doesn't hide this terrible truth from us; rather, he clearly states it for our enlightenment and preparation of things to expect. Notice what he says in **2nd Corinthians 1:8**. *"For we do not want you to be ignorant, brethren, of our trouble which came to us in Asia: that we were burdened beyond measure, above strength, so that we despaired even of life."* This is a true indication that commitment to Christ does not mean exemption from suffering.

In order to stay fully committed, we must not focus on our temporary circumstances; the focus must be on the eternal reward. Still, there will be times in your walk with the Lord that you will ask yourself the question, "What am I getting out of this?"

Chapter 13

What Am I Getting out of This?

Due to our human nature, we are leery about getting involved with anything that seems to have no benefit in it for us. Rarely, do we want to be givers without the opportunity to receive as well. This principle holds true in every aspect of our lives. It is demonstrated in our romantic relationships, personal friendships and working partnerships. Before we get involved, we want to know, what are we going to get out of it? Ultimately, we don't want to do something for nothing. To us, no apparent benefit is the same as no benefit at all.

This attitude is pervasive, even in the church. It is not always spoken but simply understood. The uncomfortable gestures and gazing looks that people give sometimes say more than words can. These are all non-verbal ways of communicating the concept that "I am not doing this for nothing."

Let us take a closer look at it from the perspective of a Believer. When we think about it realistically, we have already gotten more out of our relationship with God than we could ever give. To quote the songwriter, "You can't beat God's giving, no matter how you try." The song further states, "The more you give, the more He'll give to you. It also encourages us by saying,

"Just keep on giving because you know it's true," while speaking to the veracity of the song's lyrical content. We can count on the blessings of God because His promises are true. In fact, **2nd Corinthians 1:20** reads: *"For all the promises of God in Him are yes, and in Him Amen, to the glory of God through us."* Unlike us, because we are only human, God is trustworthy.

Just for a point of reflection, David gives us insight into this matter in the **103rd Psalm**. He pens an exhaustive list of the blessings and benefits of belonging to the family of God. In verses **2-4** he says, *"Bless the Lord oh my soul and forget not all His benefits: Who forgives all your iniquities, Who heals all your diseases, Who redeems your life from destruction, Who crowns you with loving kindness and tender mercies, Who satisfies your mouth with good things, So that your youth is renewed like the eagle's."* When you read this fascinating discovery, I believe that you would agree we are getting a great return on our investment.

There was a popular saying among the previous generation that stated, "Serving the Lord will pay off after while!" While I do not disagree with the sentiment, I believe it can be taken a bit further. By reading those previous verses, I strongly believe that serving God is paying off right now. I am a personal testimony to this fact, and I am sure that you can attest to the same with all that He has done for you. God's presence in our lives is undeniable and invokes a sense of appreciation from those of us that recognize His day to day blessings upon us.

Many times in life, we miss the obvious by looking for that which seems to be hidden from us. While we cannot deny the blessings that come from being in the house of God, we must also be fully aware of those that we reap on a daily basis. These may be missed because they seem to be insignificant or discounted as being a part of normal life. Yet, those that we fail to appreciate may be astronomical for others. Some of these are tangible and materialistic, but, the greater of them are evidenced in ways that cannot be seen but only felt and experienced.

God's greatest blessings upon your life cannot be driven, worn, eaten, slept in, or spent. The blessings of health, peace, joy, mercy, forgiveness, healing, deliverance, salvation, and, most of all, His love are priceless gifts that cannot be touched or seen. They are no less real and we experience these blessings in their fullness when we are fully committed to the things of God.

I believe that some people cannot appreciate their blessings because they really do not understand what it means to be blessed. Blessed is derived from the Greek word "makarios", which means large or lengthy. It also means fortunate or happy. As we move into the New Testament period, it becomes descriptive of one who experiences happiness due to the divine favor of God. When you begin to grasp this powerful concept, you will not just say that I am blessed and highly favored. You will live like you are.

An individual that is blessed and highly favored does not necessarily have to state it, but through their confidence, it is stated. They live in such a way that their being blessed is undeniable. We can see the personification of this in the biblical story of the virtuous woman. **Proverbs 31:28** says, *"Her children rise up and call her blessed; her husband also, and he praises her."* The volumes with which her life spoke to all who were around her are apparent in this verse. No need for a flag, a banner, a well-lit marquee, or a neon sign. Let your life speak for you.

The awesome thing about people of this caliber is not only do they recognize how blessed they are, but they also recognize the source of their blessings. **Job 10:12** states, *"You have granted me life and favor, and your care has preserved my spirit."* Therefore, the next time you need a reminder of what you are getting out of it, just read this scripture. It encompasses the unmerited blessings that we experience daily. It also opens our eyes to the fact that not only is He our provider but also our protector. It serves as a means of comfort to those who suffer from spiritual amnesia. It will bolster our confidence in God's provisional care for us and reassure us that we have nothing to worry about because He is in control.

Chapter 14

Don't Trip; I Got This!

Many of you are saying,

Although I agree with all that I have read in this book thus far, it is still hard for me to deal with my daily challenges outside of the church environment. As long as I am in the sanctuary enjoying the presence of God, my troubles seem as though they are so far away or even non-existent. But, when service is over, they seem to quickly return to mind with the administration of the benediction. It seems as though my stress level immediately escalates to an astronomical level as I anticipate the trip back home. If this sounds like you, I know the question in your mind is how do I change this? How do I get to the point where my change in location does not change my proclamation? I need to know how to put my money where my mouth is. I need to know how to demonstrate the same faith I just acted out in church. How do I move from praise, which may be performance, to practical application?

As one of God's ambassadors, if you would allow me to speak on His behave, He would say to you "Don't trip; I got this." Simply put, He is trying to get you to trust Him and know that He is in control even when it seems like He is not. I often say that you have to trust His will even when you can't trace His hand.

Even when you don't know what God is up to, know that God is up to something! Your job is to believe that He will do what is best, for your good and most of all to His glory.

Look at **Philippians 4:6**, *"Be anxious for nothing, but in everything by prayer and supplication, with thanksgiving, let your request be made known to God."* A paraphrasing of this scripture would read: Don't worry. Tell me what you need. Show some gratitude in advance (as if you know I will handle it for you) and then watch me go to work on your behalf to get you where you need to be.

This form of behavior requires a patient spirit and a confident demeanor. It takes self-restraint to refrain from trying to fix it ourselves and trying to do it our own way. Might I remind you, God does not need our help. He only needs our trust. When Jesus told His disciples, "Let not your heart be troubled," He was simply saying, "Don't trip; I got this".

When I ponder our relationship with God, it reminds me of getting in the passenger side of a car. Since we are not behind the steering wheel, we feel a sense of fear due to the fact that we are not in control. We have a tendency to shout out instructions from the passenger side. We want the driver to drive the way we want them to drive, and this may not even be the way we would drive ourselves. We want to tell the driver when to slow down (stomping on an imaginary brake pedal), speed up, stop as well as where, how, and when to turn.

Well, it begs the question: If we didn't trust the driver, why did we get in the car?

The same problems surface in our relationship with God. Many times in our prayers, we find ourselves trying to tell God when to slow down (stomping on an imaginary brake pedal), when to speed up, when to stop, and yes, even where, how, and when to turn. We would have a greater sense of peace if we realized that every situation has a beginning and an ending, neither of which we have control over. God needs us to trust Him, from the beginning to the end.

My next question to you is: Can you trust God on your way to the mountain top, even while you are in the deepest and darkest part of the valley?

The thing that we must remember is that no one quits when they are on the mountain top. They always quit while they are in the valley. That deep, dark valley represents your strains and struggles, while the mountain top symbolizes your victory. God's Word teaches us that if we allow Him to navigate us through the valley, He will ultimately get us to the mountain top. After all, the valley provides your story, (your test in testimony) while the mountain top provides God's glory.

If this was a Sunday morning worship service, I would tell you to touch your neighbor and say, "Let Him take the wheel." Then I would tell you to turn to your other neighbor and say, "Don't trip! He got this!"

When someone else is driving, we must trust that they will take us where we need to go. Even in the most difficult moments of our life, we need our faith to say, "God, I know that you will take me where I need to go." **Isaiah 42:16** states, *"I will bring the blind by a way they did not know; I will lead them to paths they have not known. I will make darkness light before them, and crooked places straight. These things I will do for them and not forsake them."* This kind of reassurance is the good news which helps Believers to become more relaxed, even when the journey gets tough.

Not only does our journey affect our attitude, but our attitude also affects our journey. Simply put, it's not only what we face but how we face it. Our attitude while we're going through is usually what makes us do what we do. Therefore, if we were to be truly honest with ourselves, we would find that no matter who we are or how regularly we worship on Sundays, we need to change our attitudes.

Chapter 15

"New and Improved"

It is amazing how companies have taken products or services that we have used and relied on for years and found a way to improve upon them. A willingness to listen, to learn, to change, and to grow led them to make their, or someone else's, product or service more successful and more effective for those that use them. These corporations did not stay stuck in the mind-set that success means completion. They continued to strive for excellence by bettering themselves. This attitude led to the new and improved version, which we all appreciate.

If this tactic works for businesses big or small in what they provide to their consumer, tell me why shouldn't it work for the people of God? If we can take this same approach to work on our attitudes, imagine the spiritual benefits we can attain.

I believe that there can be a new and improved version of us. However, one of the most detrimental factors to the success of any person or entity is the presence of a bad attitude. More often than not, it negates a willingness to change. Not only does that bad attitude have negative repercussions for that individual, but it can also have a counterproductive, infectious impact on all those connected to them.

Yes, it is possible for one bad apple to spoil the whole bunch. We see a biblical warning about this in **Galatians 5:7-9**, which reads, *"You ran well. Who hindered you from obeying the truth? This persuasion does not come from Him who calls you. A little leaven leavens the whole lump."* So, in order to remedy this problem, we must approach life, church, and God with a different attitude. Since the Believer is affiliated with all three of these components: life, church, and God, it would benefit us to use the Word of God to help us to develop a proper attitude.

We must take on an attitude of trusting in God's plan for us. This attitude of self-confidence in troubled times is solely established on a confident attitude of expectation in God during the midst of a gloomy situation. This is the description of a new and improved Believer.

This type of transformation does not come from Sunday worship alone rather from a constant and committed relationship with God, in which we realize that He can use any situation or circumstance as a tool to shape us. We see an indication of this principle in **Isaiah 64:8**, *"But now, O Lord, You are our Father; we are the clay and you are the potter; and all we are the work of Your hand."* This scripture displays an attitude of submission, which creates the opportunity for God to get the best out of us and bring out the best in us.

This reality should create an excitement in us that

cannot be extinguished. Isn't it inspiring to know that you haven't reached your peak and that the development of your new attitude brings on new blessings? After all, the new attitude itself is the greatest blessing.

Imagine how much more effective you can be in ministry, when others can see the Word of God living in your daily life and not just for 2 hours as simple performance during a church worship service on Sundays. The new and improved you can not only talk about faith for a moment, but can live it during the most difficult moments.

The greatest sermons are not those that are preached from behind the pulpit but those that are lived out in everyday experiences and require real faith and full commitment. Truthfully, many people aren't even impressed by how a preacher preaches. But, they are moved by how he lives. And, the same is or should be true of all Believers. People should be inspired by the way you live your life. One of our greatest desires should be for others to see the God in us.

We should feel that we are finally making progress, whereas when we first started off, we were merely making excuses. All our excuses do is give the devil room to come in, and even worse, offer a reason to stay. Yet, when we change our attitude, it is the same as giving him an eviction notice. It's the same as telling him what they told Mary and Joseph, the parents of Jesus, when it was time for His birth. "There is no room in the inn."

Wait a minute, not too fast. Let me caution you to beware while being reminded. **Luke 4:13** says, *"Now when the devil had ended every temptation, he departed from Him until an opportune time."* In other words, the devil is looking to make a comeback. Don't be fooled; just reading this book or any other commentary will not totally prepare you for every attack or pitfall. Don't get it twisted. These study guides only help us to look at ourselves and our relationship with God more closely and honestly.

Specifically, this book is designed to equip us with tools and techniques to help us overcome our weaknesses through our reliance on the power of our faith, understanding as well as application of God's Word, and the indwelling Holy Spirit.

There is no greater testimony to a new and improved us than the display of a disciplined, confident, and righteous lifestyle. Remember, when you practice proper behavior in Sunday service, nine times out of ten, it is only seen by other Believers. But, if you always practice proper behavior, it will help create other believers for Sunday!

You don't have to wait, until Sunday. Each new day is filled with excitement and anticipation about what God has in store for you!

Hopefully, now this strange call for Christians to Quit Living for Sunday suddenly makes sense. It is more than just a Sunday thing.

While writing this book, it helped me to face some things about myself that I need to change. Prayerfully, you have had that same revelation. That through reading and applying the principles detailed in this book, you will desire to move from being that person in Chapter 1 who lives as if they are saved for a day to that person represented in Chapter 15 who is new and improved in their attitude and behavior on a daily basis. Chapters in between 1 and 15 are the means of getting us to that powerful and profound outcome.

Most books leave you with answers. I choose to be different, because this book is about us being different. And, we are called to be different. So, I won't leave you with answers, rather two "yes or no" questions:

1. Can you see where this book has helped you identify a need for change in your attitude and behavior?

2. Do you believe that it will help move you into a better relationship with God?

If your answers are yes and yes, congratulations, mission accomplished!

The Paint Is Peeling

Pastor Norman Edmonds Sr.

COMING AT THE END OF 2016!!!

Turn to the next page for a preview of this new and exciting, follow-up book!!!

If you've ever owned anything that's gold plated, you know that sooner or later it will tell on you. Everyone who sees it will eventually discover that it's not all that it's cracked up to be. Or rather, it is what it's cracked up to be…a cheap knock off instead of the real thing.

There are too many gold plated Believers. Sadly, I must report to you that these are the ones that, in similar fashion to anything that's gilded, only sparkle when they are under the right light (ideal conditions).

As Believers, we must be careful that our Christianity isn't a thin, outer layer, which is easily worn away, to expose something less attractive and less valuable underneath. We must understand that time and circumstance will challenge the purity and quality of our relationship with God. It's not what something looks like on the outside that gives it value, but the greater measure of its value is what's on the inside.

All too often we as Believers become victims of this Multiple Layer Syndrome, and once the top coating of paint begins to peel, we are left exposed. Instead of dealing with the adverse issues that arise in our lives through cleaning or clearing them up, we try to cover them up. The only difference is our paint is a pleasant smile, make-up, and stylish clothes as well as popular scriptures and religious clichés' that we spout and/or wear on t-shirts, on bracelets, and on baseball caps.

This follow-up book will challenge us to see if we are gold platted. It will make us do some true renovations, using the Word of God, because our paint is peeling!

About The Author

Through the guidance and empowerment of the Holy Spirit, Pastor Edmonds evangelizes the lost, encourages the Believers, and equips the Saints through sound doctrine and biblical principles. Striving to positively affect everyone he encounters directly and through an extensive outreach ministry, Pastor Edmonds has become a mentor for younger pastors and ministers while also being an active agent for change in the surrounding communities. In addition, he has worked with those with developmental disabilities for the past 27 years, which he views an extension of his calling to serve. His philosophy is to remain humble and to lead by example. Through effective servant leadership, the heart of his message is: love and unity; God is love and we are one in Christ. His ministry is centered upon faith, family, and forgiveness. In everything, Pastor Edmonds gives the glory to God; for the Lord alone is worthy.

Made in the USA
Monee, IL
18 June 2025